BOOKS BY ANDREW JORON

POETRY

Trance Archive: New & Selected Poems (City Lights, 2010)

The Sound Mirror (Flood Editions, 2008)

Fathom (Black Square Editions, 2003)

The Removes (Hard Press, 1999)

Science Fiction (Pantograph Press, 1992)

Force Fields (Starmont House, 1987)

PROSE

The Cry at Zero: Selected Prose (Counterpath Press, 2007)

Neo-Surrealism; Or, The Sun at Night: Transformations of Surrealism in American Poetry, 1966-1999 (1st ed. Black Square Editions, 2004)

COLLABORATIONS

Force Fields with Brian Lucas (Hooke Press, 2010)

Invisible Machines with Robert Frazier and Thomas Wiloch (Jazz Police Books, 1993)

TRANSLATIONS

The Footsteps of One Who Has Not Stepped Forth by Richard Anders (Black Square Editions, 2000)

Literary Essays by Ernst Bloch (Stanford University Press, 1998)

EDITOR

Collected Poems of Gustaf Sobin, co-edited by Andrew Zawacki (Talisman House, 2010)

ANDREW JORON

NEO-SURREALISM
OR, THE
SUN
AT NIGHT

TRANSFORMATIONS OF
SURREALISM IN AMERICAN POETRY
1966—1999

KOLOURMEIM PRESS
OAKLAND, CA
TRANS·MARK

Neo-Surrealism; or, the Sun at Night previously appeared as a chapter of *The World in Time and Space: Towards a History of American Innovative Poetry in Our Time*, edited by Edward Foster and Joseph Donahue (Talisman House, 2002). An expanded version of the essay appeared as a chapbook from Black Square Editions in 2004. This newly expanded version is the second, revised edition.

Book design and layout by Jeff Mellin (jeffmellin.com)

ISBN 9780615323693

Kolourmeim Press

El Kolourmeim, Publisher

NEO-SURREALISM OR, THE SUN AT NIGHT

Surrealism is the practice

OF CONJURING OTHERNESS,

OF REALIZING THE INFINITE NEGATIVITY OF DESIRE IN ORDER TO ADDRESS, AND TO REDRESS, THE POVERTY OF THE POSITIVE FACT. IN MARXIAN TERMS, IT DEMANDS A SENSORIUM, A SOCIAL BODY, CAPABLE OF MAKING THE LEAP FROM THE REALM OF NECESSITY TO THE REALM OF FREEDOM.

The surrealist identification of reality and desire has obvious sources in Romanticism and even earlier, alchemical and Hermetic, doctrines. However, in surrealism this identification leads, not to reconciliation, but to agonistic embrace—that is, to the beautiful convulsion of irresolvable paradox. For surrealism, the vertiginous spiral by which the familiar is estranged can never end in refamiliarization. The surrealist struggle has to be waged not only against society but also, scandalously, against nature. Its cosmo-political teaching heralds the establishment of a Church of Disquiet.

Still, surrealism does not levitate above History; the shape of surrealist subversion shifts according to the contours of the surrounding landscape. Both the darkness of the "uncanny" and the brightness of the "marvellous" are not absolute but relative qualities. Only at midnight does the apparition of the Sun become strange.

As Philip Lamantia, the most prominent North American surrealist, has asked: "What is not strange?" The question raises the curtain on the situation of surrealism in the New World, where everything—and so nothing—is strange. Here, in the society of the spectacle, the empowering twist of estrangement tends to reverse direction and spiral toward the passive doom of alienation. Here, the techniques of surrealism seem to have been all too readily absorbed by the advertising system.

Yet in the Old World also, surrealism was implicated in—even as it developed a radical response to—the increasing commodification of the life-world. Surrealism has enacted, since its inception, a critique and a carnival of the object under capitalism. And in doing so, it has anticipated and transcended the self-ironizing discourse of postmodern consumerism: for the object is not simply a sign to be endlessly circulated, but also a *non-sign*, the materialization of a mystery whose *non-sense* signals the irruption of the genuinely new.

In the dominant culture of the United States, otherness has been systematically denied a presence, so that the surreal must be perceived only as a representation of the unreal. Perhaps this is why those postwar American artists who fell under the influence of surrealism—Gorky, Motherwell, Pollock—tended, in their later practice, to redefine the problem of representation itself, and to reclaim the will-to-otherness as a form of the non-representational.

(No similar stratagem was undertaken by the surrealist-inspired poets of that time: Parker Tyler's verse, for example, never ventured far from Romantic metaphor. In some sense, however, an impulse toward abstraction was already evident in the most "advanced" surrealist

ANDREW JORON

poetry, where the imagery—the juxtaposition, according to Breton's famous citation of Reverdy, of "the most distant realities"—remains properly non-visualizable.)

The postwar moment was altogether a fateful one for the reception of surrealism in the United States. Breton and his associates, during their years of exile in New York, had encouraged the formation of an American surrealist community. After Breton's return to Paris, however, the American surrealists were left leaderless and soon dispersed. By 1945, *VVV* and *View*—magazines that were vehicles for the group's art and writing—had ceased publication. As Charles Henri Ford, editor of View and the most accomplished American surrealist poet of his day, complained, "There's no place to sleep in this bed, Tanguy." The art historian Dickran Tashjian, in his monograph *A Boatload of Madmen: Surrealism and the American Avant-garde 1920–1950*, asserts that "the Surrealists were effaced from the American record even while significant traces lingered in the wake of their departure." Tashjian further states that "the Surrealists were banished from the American cultural terrain, both at the outset and at the conclusion of their encounters with American artists and writers."

As orthodox surrealism receded, however, it began to glow: it now became a part of the "background radiation" of American culture. Enough of its light leaked through the fifties' and early sixties' atmosphere of conformism and conservatism to color the writings of the Ashbery, O'Hara, Spicer (whose *After Lorca* stands as one of the finest exemplars of American neo-surrealism) and the Beats.

In the second volume of the anthology Tracts surréalistes et déclarations collectives, the French surrealist José Pierre periodized the fortunes of surrealism during the fifties and sixties as follows: "The Traversal of the Desert," 1952–1958; "The Resurgence," 1959–1965; and "The Hour of the Phoenix," 1966–1969. Certainly, the rising tide of oppositional activity in the sixties promoted such a resurgence. The situationists and other radical groups explicitly cited surrealism; its influence seemed to expand in proportion to the intensity of the struggle against imperialist war and the one-dimensionality of capitalist society (the slogans of the May '68 student revolt in Paris, such as "L'imagination prend le pouvoir," "Je prends mes désirs pour des réalités car je crois en la réalité de mes désirs," "Explorons le hasard," recall passages from the first and second Manifestoes). The mystical, apocalyptic, and psychedelic tendencies of sixties counterculture also mingled with political currents, adding momentum to the surrealist surge in America. The time-line shows a sharp clustering of such works between the mid sixties and the early seventies: Lamantia's *Touch of the Marvelous* (1966) and *Selected Poems* (1967); Sotère Torregian's *The Golden Palomino Bites the Clock* (1966); Louis Hammer's *Bone Planet* (1967); George Hitchcock's *The Dolphin with the Revolver in Its Teeth* (1967); Bill Knott's *The Naomi Poems: Corpse and Beans* (1968), whose subtitle alludes to Desnos's *Corps et biens*; Franklin Rosemont's *The Morning of a Machine Gun* (1968); Lamantia's *Blood of the Air* (1970); Pete Winslow's *Mummy Tapes* (1971); Torregian's *The Wounded Mattress* (1970); and Winslow's *A Daisy in the Memory of a Shark* (1973). There was thus some cause to celebrate the phoenix-like rebirth of an authentic surrealist poetry, even at the hour of Breton's death (which occurred in 1966).

In 1970, *Radical America* (the organ of the revolutionary Students for a Democratic Society) devoted a special issue to surrealism. The issue's guest editor, Franklin Rosemont, stated in his introduction that "surrealism fully recognizes that the liberation of the mind requires thoroughgoing social liberation (that is, the emancipation of the working class) and consequently situates itself unhesitatingly in the service of the Revolution." True to its setting within the oppositional and sometimes utopian culture of the time, the rebirth of surrealist poetry in the United States was accompanied by the issuance of manifestos, the staging of art exhibitions, protests, and happenings, and the launching of new movements and organizations. These proved to be more or less ephemeral, with one notable exception: the activities of Chicago Surrealist Group. Founded in 1966 by Franklin and Penelope

Rosemont, the group has, up to the present day, promulgated a militantly orthodox brand of Bretonian surrealism through the publication of over two hundred pamphlets and chapbooks and an assortment of perfect-bound books. Over the decades, the group has suffered from a largely self-imposed insularity; according to a statement in the third issue of the group's periodical *Arsenal* (1976), "we do not collaborate on bourgeois literary and artistic reviews, preferring to present our researches in our own publications where the integrity and scope of the surrealist project are not compromised by the abject opportunist deceit characteristic of the cultural racket.... The only possible exceptions might be in cases in which an entire issue, or a large section of a publication was placed at our disposal, carte blanche, under our exclusive editorship." The sterilizing effects of such a puristic, if not puritanical, stance is revealed in the formulaic quality of much of the group's poetry (it is instructive to compare their work with that of the "unaffiliated" neo-surrealist poets who arose in the seventies and later). The poetic practice of the Chicago Group seems flattened by the massive and inescapable presence of the ur-texts of "classical" surrealism. (Yet there are moments of originality in the poems of group member Joseph Jablonski: see his collections *In a Moth's Wing* [1974] and *The Dust on My Eyes Is the Blood of Your Hair* [1980].) In general, the group's program consists of an all-too-familiar compound of aesthetic conservatism and political radicalism.

But surrealism is not exempt from its own imperative, synthesized from Marx and Rimbaud, to "transform the world" and to "change life." Even in its earliest years, while unified under the leadership of Breton, the movement underwent successive mutations in response to internal and external conditions. The self-identity of the movement therefore cannot be situated within timeless tenets, but only in the shock-pattern of the wave-front of surrealization as it passes, under the impetus of practices not to be prescribed in advance, through a particular time and place. This expanding wave-front has no permanently fixed form or content. Surreality is not a state of standing "over" reality; rather, it is the boiling-over of that reality, a phase-change that always departs from a highly specific set of initial conditions. "Neo-surrealism" is a term that refuses termination—one that awaits the emergence of the *novum* within surrealism itself.

Lamantia once, in the very pages of *Arsenal*, articulated a neo-surrealist position in his statement "Between the Gulfs" (1973): "From this vista of dormant volcanos and tropical ice, we can all the more happily trace our inspirations from Lautréamont and Rimbaud to Breton and Péret and Roussel to [the Haitian poet] Magloire-Saint-Aude, exemplary signposts for further transgressions, without literally re-tracing in one's own poetic praxis their inimitable movements [emphasis added]." In the context of the Chicago Surrealist Group's own rather imitative poetry, these words seem to offer a subtle hint of reproof. At the same time, Lamantia has supported the activities of the group by contributing to their publications and co-signing many of their collective declarations.

Despite the shortcomings of some of their verse, the Chicago Surrealist Group continues to perform valuable work across a wide spectrum; they are undeniably one of the most important sources of surrealist thought and practice in the United States. They were among the first to translate and disseminate many of the works of "classic" French surrealism; they have maintained contacts with other surrealist groups around the world, as well as with radical historians and labor activists; and they have delved deeply into the popular culture of the United States to discover the "accomplices of surrealism." For example, Paul Garon's *Blues and the Poetic Spirit* (Da Capo Press, 1975) is a knowledgeable and affecting study of the poetry of the blues from a surrealist perspective. As for the presentation of classical surrealism, the 536-page compendium What Is Surrealism? Selected Writings of André Breton (Pluto Press, 1978), edited by Franklin Rosemont, remains one of the most comprehensive editions of Breton's texts available in English.

Most recently, Penelope Rosemont has edited a sizeable anthology of Women Surrealists (University of Texas Press, 1998). The anthology, which contains poetry, essays, fiction, and artwork, is international in scope. The American contingent, however, is (with the exception of Rikki Ducornet and Jayne Cortez) represented by minor poets, associates of the Chicago group itself. Nonetheless, the anthology's documentation of surrealist work by women beyond these shores is thorough and meticulous.

The Rosemonts' claim to represent the true and authentic lineage of surrealism in the United States is, in fact, a considerable one: they were the last American poets to receive any measure of recognition from Breton (on a trip to Paris in 1966, they were "welcomed by Breton into the surrealist movement"). Such recognition was also extended to Lamantia in 1943, but he has shown far less inclination to organize a homegrown movement than the Rosemonts (who were labor activists in their youth). Lamantia was always too self-absorbed for such work, too attentive to his inner transformations: his self-described "mystical silences" and experiments with hallucinogenic drugs give evidence of this. Indeed, the two faces of French surrealism—one looking exoterically outward to political and cultural revolution, the other looking esoterically inward to spiritual revelation—seem to be reflected in the complementarity of the Rosemonts' and Lamantia's respective approaches to American surrealism.

Lamantia (who was born in San Francisco in 1927) first encountered surrealism as a freshman in high school, at an art exhibit featuring the paintings of Miró and Dali. His first poems were published in the magazine View when he was fifteen years old. The young poet then initiated a correspondence with Breton, who at that time was residing in New York. Breton hailed him as "a voice that rises once in a hundred years." In early 1944, Lamantia's poem "Touch of the Marvelous," along with his letters to Breton, appeared in the final issue of VVV. Lamantia dropped out of high school and traveled to New York, where he met Breton, Charles Henri Ford, Parker Tyler, and other American and European surrealists; eventually, he joined the editorial staff of View. With the dispersal of the New York surrealists at the end of World War II, Lamantia went home to finish high school. Subsequently, he attended classes (though never officially enrolled) at the University of California at Berkeley. Here, he took part in radical political activities but also became preoccupied with occult lore, gnosticism, and other traditions of religious heresy. Two years later he abandoned academia to wander around the world. His travels led him through the American Southwest, Mexico, and finally overseas to France and Morocco. While on the move, he continued to write and submit his work for publication; his first book, *Erotic Poems*, was issued in 1946 by Bern Porter. During this decade of wandering, Lamantia returned occasionally to San Francisco and New York, where he immersed himself in the jazz scene and associated with Beat writers. Lamantia's Beat-inflected poems from this period are assembled in *Ekstasis* and *Destroyed Works*, both published by Auerhahn Press in San Francisco. The following lines from "Hypodermic Light" (included in the latter collection) illustrate Lamantia's ongoing quest for ecstatic, often drug-mediated, mystical experience in non-Western cultures and in the West's own pre-capitalist culture:

My friend keeps talking in my head of magic herb
Colombian Indians snort, shut their eyes seeing clouds and
float around like clouds
I'm looking for the seeds of the Virgin.

In the early fifties, the poet participated in the peyote rituals of the Washo tribe of Native Americans. For Lamantia, who had been raised as a Catholic, the seeds of ecstatic experience are also scattered through the heretical traditions of the Church: he is depicted shooting up before an altar on the cover of *Narcotica* (a polemic against repressive drug laws with supplementary texts by Artaud, published in 1959 by Auerhahn Press).

In the early sixties, Lamantia temporarily stopped writing: this was the period of his "mystical orientations & silences." He resumed his wanderings through Europe, living in Spain, Italy, and Greece. In the meantime, his earliest poems were reprinted in *Touch of the Marvelous* by Berkeley's Oyez Press, and his *Selected Poems 1943–1966* was published by City Lights in San Francisco. The latter volume showed a progression from dreamy eroticism in the forties through the fifties' Beat attitude (with its jazzy, bedraggled, bedrugged beatitude) to the more controlled and authoritative esoterism of the work that, after 1963, emerged from the silences. Lamantia's return to writing—and, more than ever, to a surrealism in the service of the Revelation—was confirmed by the release of *The Blood of the Air* at the turn of the decade. One reviewer in *Poetry* (Chicago) observed that the collection marked "a return to surrealism, but to a different surrealism.... The concept of the 'adept' is repeated throughout and there are many references to alchemy, Egyptian mythology, and the Middles Ages."

In Lamantia's mature work, language often functions in the manner of esoteric texts, by using words as hermetic seals to simultaneously conceal and mark the location of power sources. Such allusive, elusive strategies were developed by medieval and Renaissance mages to insure that the fruits of the Great Work would not fall into hands of the uninitiated. In *The Blood of the Air*, Lamantia appropriates these strategies as a sign of poetic empowerment: "All the mancies shall be mine who grew the trunk from the vibrated seed sent from the sun," he vows in the prose poem "World without End." He also proclaims that "I am salved with the unflickering beacon roaring from the magenta whorl floating through the veil of Hermes Trismegistus, the original voice come from under the wink of 40 centuries." Lamantia's renewed purpose in writing, then, is not to lift the "veil of Hermes" (which would constitute a betrayal of that hermetic knowledge kept secret for "40 centuries"); rather, it is to announce that the "original voice" of Hermes now inhabits the poet, that a transmission, a transmutation, has taken place.

> treasure shored up from my inner eyes
> the victuals medieval cathedrals secrete secretly

for the likes of the adepts
who smile through the velvet fissures of the centuries
that are Waves & Blankets of Stars
under which we are given, if we burrow long enough
for the hidden script, the Key to the King's Shut Chamber
that vanishes into the night hot with luminations. . .

In this language of correspondences (which provides the infrastructure for magical efficacy), nothing occupies the place of the referent but another sign. The meaning of the mystery always recedes and "vanishes into the night hot with luminations." This revelation has no content but conjuration: it is the mage's own movement within an infinity of facing mirrors that makes the poem.

During the seventies, Lamantia increasingly invoked the natural history of the Far West and the lore of its indigenous peoples, interpreting these as a system of sacred signs, alongside traditional Western esoteric sources such as the cabala. In the poem "Redwood Highway," for example, Lamantia divines "the coming of cursive script on the Micmac barks" and "a star field of birds / whose cries paint the sonorous language." As Foucault noted of Renaissance discourse, "These buried similitudes must be indicated on the surface of things; there must be visible marks for the invisible analogies." Accordingly, Lamantia's lines might be characterized as a delirious cataloging of the "visible marks" of "invisible analogies"; his poems of the seventies were collected in a volume entitled *Becoming Visible*, published in 1981 by City Lights.

Throughout the 1980s, Lamantia continued to apply his esoteric learning to the biosphere of the West Coast and especially to the magical alphabet of its birds. "There are many centers of mystic geography," Lamantia wrote at this time, "but the great Black V of gold flashing in the meadow Bird unknown / opening the air like all the lore of the chants," that avian V whose form resembles that of an open book, had become for him the most potent of signs, the most visible mark of the invisible. Thus, Lamantia utilizes a Renaissance model of reading as interpretation of the cascade of correspondences, as translation of the mirror-signs reflecting the light of an invisible Original. His readings of the Far West's biosphere culminate in *Meadowlark West*, a collection published by City Lights in 1986. Here, for example, is his gloss on a Northern California mountain peak:

Shasta great Shasta
Lemurian dream island, perhaps Atlantis, scallop on the
    sierras, Hopi sovereign of animate dream, oceanic claw:
    Alta California climbs into view.
Shasta great Shasta
geography in a mystic state later pruned by seers.

In 1989, Lamantia undertook a journey to Egypt, the very source of the occult tradition: next to his love for the life and landscape of the West, he has long been impassioned by the mythology and learning of Egypt, as well as by all varieties of para-Egyptology. In more than one poem of this period, Lamantia superimposes "the great signature / that is eternal Egypt" upon his native ground: "the temple of Luxor goes over it in a transparency to catch it before it goes A Vision of Synarchic Bioregions over Northern California's haunted scapes." More and more, the texts of Lamantia's poems have been composed of layerings of esoteric citations, oracular archaeologies: consequently, the mature Lamantian poem may be defined as a "Bed of Sphinxes." In 1997, City Lights issued a volume of Lamantia's new and selected poems under this title (the book contains six new poems, including "Egypt" and "Passionate Ornithology Is Another Kind of Yoga").

Like Lamantia's (and Franklin Rosemont's) earlier work, the writings of San Francisco poet Pete Winslow negotiate the passageway between Beat poetry and surrealism. Winslow died suddenly in 1972, aged 37. While Winslow's style, especially in his last years, had been moving toward a space of grace and clarity comparable to that of

Eluard's *Capital of Pain*, many of his published works rely on a jazzy, jagged rhythm of incantatory refrains:

> The old and the new collide every couple of billion years
> Striking sparks which set the mind racing
> Sparks of feasting on the charred flesh of one's comfort
> Sparks of triumphal entry into snow castles. . .
> Sparks of people speaking the crazy thoughts of a fish
> Sparks of new fruits the same as the old except
> > for the writing inside. . .

Winslow seems to have felt the tension between "the old and the new" within surrealism as well. In an essay published in 1971, he denounced certain American poets for attempting to "redefine" surrealism; Winslow argued that Breton's definition of surrealism as "pure psychic automatism" was "still applicable." According to Winslow, "It is simple enough to adhere to Breton's definition unless one is swayed by esthetic or moralistic concerns, or by the desire to please the makers of literary reputations." Winslow's only widely distributed book, *A Daisy in the Memory of a Shark* (City Lights, 1973), was posthumously published.

Bob Kaufman, a black surrealist and Beat-associated poet who for many years lived in San Francisco, was never acknowledged by Breton or the members of the Chicago Surrealist Group. The literary scholar Charles Nyland has commented that Kaufman's surrealism "is not Breton's automatic writing. It appears to be logically derived from his awareness of paradox and discontinuity and from experimenting with bebop and black speech patterns."

> In black core of night, it explodes
> Silver thunder, rolling back my brain,
> Bursting copper screens, memory worlds
> Deep in star-fed beds of time,

Seducing my soul to diamond fires of night.
Faint outline, a ship—momentary fright
Lifted on waves of color,
Sunk in pits of light,
Drummed back through time,
Hummed back through mind,
Drumming, cracking the night.

Kaufman was born in New Orleans in 1925 (his father was half African American, half Jewish; his mother was Creole); as a young man, he traveled to New York and found work as a merchant seaman. There, he also became involved in leftist politics and the jazz scene. After Kaufman married, he renounced sea-voyaging and settled in San Francisco, where he was soon caught up in the oppositional current of the Beats. According to some witnesses, Kaufman assumed the role of a political agitator among the Beat poets, stirring them to action with fiery rants that often sounded like a kind of improvisatory "jazz canto." By the end of the fifties, he was helping to produce the mimeo-graphed magazine *Beatitude* (now regarded as a quintessential emanation of the Beat movement), and his first collection, *Solitudes Crowded with Loneliness*, had been published by New Directions.

In a radio interview, one of Kaufman's friends stated that "Bob's main concern was the revolution. His poetry was a revolutionary germ that was functioning in people's psyches to transform them. And so I think that he was always concerned with transforming his own psyche." Kaufman was in fact a virtuoso practitioner of the Rimbaldian precept of "disordering the senses"; he was jailed more than once for his subversive disorderliness. He returned to New York in the early sixties, but was back in San Francisco on the eve of Kennedy's assassination. In response to that event, Kaufman fell into a state of quasi-silence (speaking rarely, and then only in monosyllables) that lasted for ten years—an indication not only of Kaufman's sensitivity, but also of the overwhelming signifi-cance with which he endowed the act of speech.

Kaufman's poetry originated as oral art, as inspired utterance that was only occasionally transcribed and preserved, either by himself or others. It is poetry that trembles with innocence and outrage, anxiety and exultation all mingling in equal measure. It has the strength and vulnerability of work that has just barely (and only temporarily) escaped catastrophe: "The Ancient Rain has moved me to another world, where the people stand still and the streets moved me to destination. I look down on the Earth and see myself wandering in the Ancient Rain, ecstatic, aware that the death I feel around me is in the hands of the Ancient Rain and those who plan death for me and dreams are known to the Ancient Rain... silent, humming raindrops of the Ancient Rain." The manuscript of *The Ancient Rain* (a collection published by New Directions in 1981) was rescued by friends from a burned-out hotel room that Kaufman had been forced to abandon.

Kaufman's poetic speech was always a form of direct address, whether his interlocuter was another person or the inhuman face of Time itself (at such moments, Kaufman's gaze resembles that of Klee's wide-eyed Angel of the New, blown away by history's vast explosion). Yet, despite its frequently anxious, anguished tone, Kaufman's work is also pervaded by a brash and biting humour noir; his "Abomunist Manifesto" satirizes the rhetoric attributed to political and aesthetic vanguard movements. Here, the poet becomes a trickster figure whose willingness to destabilize his own foundations is, paradoxically enough, an important source of his power over reality (a source, in other words, of his surreality).

Ginsberg has related that "Simon Watson Taylor, the pataphysician and translator [of Breton's Surrealism and Painting, among other works], would make a point every time he went to San Francisco of seeing Kaufman. And I think Kaufman was the only poet that Taylor felt really had a true surrealist muse... He was always totally respectful of Kaufman as being the great surrealist American poet." Kaufman's own surrealist self-portrait, in his poem "I Am a Camera," presents an iconic, ironic picture of the poet's paradoxical state of being:

THE POET NAILED ON
THE HARD BONE OF THIS WORLD,
HIS SOUL DEDICATED TO SILENCE
IS A FISH WITH FROG'S EYES,
THE BLOOD OF A POET FLOWS
OUT WITH HIS POEMS, BACK
TO THE PYRAMID OF BONES
FROM WHICH HE IS THRUST
HIS DEATH IS A SAVING GRACE

CREATION IS PERFECT

Bob Kaufman, shortly before his death, entered a North Beach bar and proclaimed (according to Neeli Cherkovski), "I have seen my own death. One day I shall be walking down Grant Avenue. And a pay telephone will ring. I will pick it up. It will be Jean Cocteau on the other end. And he will say, 'The Blood of the Poet.'" In 1986, Kaufman died of emphysema in San Francisco; a volume of selected poems, *Cranial Guitar*, was published by Coffee House in 1996.

Another American surrealist poet of African—and, in this case, Arab—ancestry who has never been accorded recognition by "orthodox" surrealist groups is Sotère Torregian, author of six poetry collections published between 1966 and 1979 (although Lamantia once hailed him as a "brother surrealist," Winslow later accused Torregian of revisionism). Torregian was born in 1941, grew up in New Jersey, and associated with poets of the New York School in the early sixties. In 1967, Torregian moved to California, where he taught as writer in residence at Stanford University from 1969 to 1973, and assisted in launching the Afro-American Studies program there in 1969. He has attested to the influence of both the French surrealists and "the poets of Négritude (Senghor and Césaire)." His two most important publications—*The Wounded Mattress* (Oyez Press, 1968) and *The Age of Gold*

(Kulchur Foundation, 1976)—reveal a wry absurdist humorousness, a delicate, sometimes fairy-tale-like lyricism, and a lively eroticism.

Moreover, Torregian exhibits a courtly-Romantic consciousness of the poem as gift, as cornucopia to be shared within a privileged circle of creative spirits. In *The Age of Gold*, many poems are addressed and dedicated to other poets, musicians, artists, family members, and film actresses: the marvellous enters by way of a series of "impossible" recognitions set free inside the mirrors of intersubjectivity. In a poem "For an Unknown Princess," Torregian writes that "The Poet and the gunman arrested in your reflection are one." And in a one-line poem "For Joe Ceravolo and Mona Da Vinci," he writes "I sleep in you Great House that sleeps." Torregian's work is most often situated here, in the Great House of the Earth, many-mansioned with oceanic awareness, multi-storied with meditations on—and mediations of—human being. Torregian's version of surrealism transmogrifies the desire for otherness into desire for the Other. During the eighties, Torregian ceased to publish his work following a succession of personal hardships. In 1999, his chapbook Always for the First Time was published jointly by Kolourmeim and Pantograph Press. And the Austin-based press Skanky Possum released a perfectbound edition of Torregian's selected works from 1957 to 1999, entitled *I Must Go (She Said) Because My Pizza's Cold.*

The work of two other African-American poets, Ted Joans and Jayne Cortez, while often labelled "jazz poetry," also bears the strong imprint of surrealism. (After the Beats, many American surrealist poets have claimed inspiration from jazz—a tendency that diverges interestingly from the French surrealists' silence on the question of music.)

Ted Joans's poetic pathway can be traced through the Beat era (when he lived in Greenwich Village and associated with Ginsberg, Kerouac, and Kaufman), the black arts movement, and surrealism. Since the early sixties (when he became an expatriate, restlessly shifting his residence between various cities throughout Europe and Africa), Joans has showed a sustained interest in surrealism; his letters to Breton were printed in a French literary magazine in 1963. The critic Jon Woodson has characterized Joans's poetry as "a vehicle for social protest.... Ted Joans is a poet of the people who has used the jazz idiom to create a style of poetry that has gained wide popular acceptance because of its fluidity, honesty, and vitality." At the same time, Joans's declamatory lines, despite their vehemence and verve, rarely rise to the pitch of the unprecedented: "Under the hot frosted bed I saw / a mangled trumpet that Dizz never blew and never wished to." Among Joans's more surrealist-oriented writings are *Flying Piranha* (co-authored with the French surrealist Joyce Mansour, and published by New York's Bola Press in 1978) and *Some Sum of Surrealist Poems* (published by Letters, a Toronto small press, in 1987). Ted Joans died in 2003.

Compared to Joans's predictable jazziness, Jayne Cortez's fire-spitting musicality defies all expectation. Wide awake with the exacting rhythms of an exalted rage, her work shakes the body—and consequently the mind—loose from the somnolence of received forms. So that surrealism's surprising leaps are marshalled to perform a choreography of revolutionary violence:

> When i blow open green bottles
> straight across hump of a frozen tongue
>
> when i shove brown glass
> through the skull of a possum
> and pass from my ears a baptism of red piss
>
> when i cry from my butt like a jackal
> and throw limbs of a dying mule into the river...
>
> when my mystical bunions
> like steel hearses jam eyes
> into searching spit of a starving wolf
> into cosmic lips like monkey genitals...

I see a way through the maroon glass of this milky way
I say i see a way through for the cradle of hulls
sticking through these indigo ankles
I see a way through. . .

Even in the first-person singular, Cortez's voice often sounds like a chorus. Her Pan-African imagination opens outward to a polyphony of mythic remappings, to where the poet's solar sensorium can "see a way through" the univocal night of economic, sexual, and racial oppression. The poetry of Cortez calls up an implacable energy that surrounds its adversary like "a circle of signifying snakes."

Jayne Cortez was born in 1936 in Arizona and grew up in the Watts district of Los Angeles; later, she moved to New York City. For a time, she was married to the innovative jazz composer and saxophonist Ornette Coleman; she herself has led a jazz group named the Firespitters (in which the instrumentalists provide accompaniment for her recitation of poetry; the group has released several albums). Cortez's books include *Scarifications* (Bola Press, 1973), *Firespitter* (Bola Press, 1982), *Coagulations: New and Selected Poems* (Thunder's Mouth Press, 1984), *Poetic Magnetic* (Bola Press, 1991), and *Somewhere in Advance of Nowhere* (High Risk Books, 1996).

Cortez's far-from-doctrinal surrealism derives mostly from that of Césaire and the other poets of the Négritude movement. (In the cultural context of the United States, not surprisingly, the surrealism of Aimé Césaire—with demotic, demonic sources—can seem more relevant and convincing than that of the Old-World patrician André Breton.)

Surrealism has entered the United States from more than one direction. Other lineages of "non-Parisian" surrealism (in addition to the Caribbean branch) have assumed importance here: an allegorizing Eastern European mode of surrealism is apparent in the work of Charles Simic, for example. And the "deep-image" poets of the sixties and seventies preferred Neruda's Latin-American surrealism to the Rimbaldian "derangements" of the French tradition.

Robert Kelly, in 1961, invented the term "deep image" to emphasize that the image in poetic language is a projection from the depths of the ego (as modelled by the depth psychology of Freud and Jung). Kelly, together with Robert Bly and Jerome Rothenberg, advocated a poetics of the "new imagination," based in part on advances made by the European and Latin-American avant-garde (especially surrealism) in realizing inner experience by means of the "image." As Rothenberg explained it, the deep image is "an exploration of the unconscious region of the mind in such a way that the unconscious [of the poet] is speaking to the unconscious [of the reader]." In the words of Bly's former protégé Gregory Orr: "When, in conjunction with his trans-lating, Bly affirmed what he called 'the image' (and which has since acquired the critical label, 'deep image'), he was attempting to reunite American poetry with the mainstream developments of Romantic po-etry as it had evolved on the European mainland: a poetry structured by symbolic imagination and making extensive (Neruda, surrealism) or intensive (Rilke, Tranströmer) use of symbols."

These notions, while sharing some superficial affinities with sur-realism, nevertheless fall short of surrealism's radical demand for the dialectical Aufhebung of dream and reality. The deep imagists tended to rely on the "intensification of intuition" (citing Jung) rather than on the intensification of contradiction; theirs was essentially an affir-mative art, devoid of the surrealist appetite for negation and otherness (as exemplified by Breton's phrase "Existence is elsewhere"). Indeed, Bly, according to his literary biographer Richard P. Sugg, rejected the "goal of derangement characteristic of the French tradition" and "con-trasted this goal with that of the so-called new surrealism, as practiced by poets of the new imagination such as James Wright, Neruda, and himself, poets who disregard the conscious, intellectual structure of the mind entirely and, [in Bly's words,] 'by the use of images, try to bring forward another reality from inward experience.'"

In spite of their anti-surrealist subjectivism, the practitioners of the deep image are often regarded as the major American inheritors of surrealism. Yet the failure of the deep image as a mode of experimentation (that is, its eventual reconciliation with New-Critical techniques in the form of "academic workshop" poetry) seems to have poisoned the roots of surrealism itself for many poets of the American avant-garde. Even so, from the late fifties through the eighties, dangerously "deranging" forms of surrealism and neo-surrealism could, and did, find support within the ambit of deep-image publications and interests. Thus, in the pages of Bly's periodical series *The Fifties*, *The Sixties*, and *The Seventies*, translations of European and Latin American surrealist texts were published along with uncompromising new work by indigenous (neo-)surrealists such as Philip Lamantia and Bill Knott.

The most sustained, and most visible, interaction between deep-image and surrealist poetry occurred in the pages of *kayak*, a magazine edited by George Hitchcock (himself a surrealist poet of some distinction). In the first nineteen issues, an introductory statement proclaimed hospitality to "surrealist, imagist, and political poems." (Although the statement was dropped from subsequent issues, the editorial policy continued.) *Kayak* was a magazine wholly infused with the style and personality of its editor; over the course of its 64 issues (published between 1964 and 1984), it remained remarkably consistent both in its aesthetic orientation and its appearance (staple-bound, with "distressed" typography, colored inks and paper, and Ernst-like collages). The magazine had a rough-and-ready elegance , like Hitchcock's own poetry. Sometimes, the collages and colorations that were integral to *kayak*'s design seemed to outperform the texts themselves, playfully creeping and seeping into the magazine's poetic content.[1]

---

1   After *kayak* ceased publication in 1984, its commitment to surrealism was inherited most visibly by *Caliban*, a literary magazine edited by Lawrence R. Smith. Fifteen issues of the magazine appeared between 1986 and 1995 and featured work by many of *kayak*'s former contributers, as well as fostering work by post-*kayak* neo-surrealists such as George Kalamaras and Will Alexander.

ANDREW JORON

The cohabitation of surrealism and imagism was not always easy: in one instance, Bly, a regular contributor, criticized (at Hitchcock's invitation!) what he considered to be *kayak*'s "formulaic" surrealism—and was met by a vigorous response on the part of the magazine's surrealist partisans. In other instances, a few poets managed to effect a certain rapprochement between the two practices—as, for example, in the work of Bert Meyers, who saw "All around me, butterflies, / ecstatic hinges, / hunt for the ideal door," and that of John Haines, who heard "the sound / of moonlight breaking, / of brittle stars ground together." Yet somehow such truces seemed fragile and temporary, even within the space of a single poem—for the "elsewhere" of surrealism tended to escape from the entrapping (subjectivizing) pathos of a poetics based on "inwardness."

Hitchcock's own poetry itself possesses the charm and perhaps the quaintness of a handworked artifact: many of its images seem deliberately drawn from a sepia-toned inventory of obsolescent objects. In one poem, "Figures in a Ruined Ballroom,"

> The chandeliers hemorrhage, Tritons
> weep for the plaster dolphins, the pheasant
> in its glass room feeds on candle-droppings:
>
> apothecaries cannot heal the wax dogs,
> sutures will no longer save Apollo
> nor violins awake the stuffed ospreys.

The poem's final lines are "These statues turn by concealed levers: / their hinges fold in on mortality." Hitchcock's poetry thus embodies an aspect of surrealism that treats the past—especially the recent past—as a storehouse of the unconscious, where all that is half-submerged, caught in the act of (material or memorial) disappearance, seems pregnant with unrealized meaning. As Walter Benjamin pointed out in his essay on surrealism, the Parisian surrealists were the "first to perceive the revolutionary energies that appear in the 'outmoded,' in the first iron constructions, the first factory buildings, the earliest photos, the objects that have begun to be extinct, grand pianos, the dresses of five years ago, fashionable restaurants when the vogue has begun to ebb from them." That such uncanny alignments of lost and last things can still become conduits for poetic (if not revolutionary) energy is repeatedly demonstrated in the delicately crafted, almost miniaturist, works of Hitchcock.

Before becoming a lecturer at the University of California at Santa Cruz, Hitchcock labored at such artisanal trades as shipbuilding and landscaping. Hitchcock's age (he was born in 1914, one year later than Charles Henri Ford) places him among the first generation of American surrealists—however, Hitchcock's writings did not begin to appear until the fifties. His later books of poetry include Lessons in Alchemy (West Coast Poetry Review, 1976), The Piano Beneath the Skin (Copper Canyon, 1978), Mirror on Horseback (Kayak Books, 1979), and The Wounded Alphabet: Poems Collected and New, 1953–1983 (Jazz Press/Papabach Editions, 1984).

Hitchcock's "artisanal surrealism" seems congruent with what the critic Walter Kalaidjian has called "the deep image's pastoral surrealism"—which, with "its authentic privacy and its psychic distance from everyday life, bespeak a profound unease with America's social milieu." Among the deep imagists of the sixties and seventies, this sense of unease was often represented by pre-industrial landscapes and tableaux, in order, perhaps, to be better translated into a timeless, metaphysical discourse. One of the poets who has most successfully synthesized imagism and surrealism, and whose work is also strongly pervaded by the melancholic mood of the "outmoded," is Charles Simic, a regular contributor to kayak (his first two collections of poetry were published by Kayak Books). In "A Landscape with Crutches," Simic describes

The bread on its artificial limbs,
A headless doll in a wheelchair,

ANDREW JORON

And my mother, mind you, using
Two knives for crutches as she squats to pee.

Simic was born in the Serbian region of Yugoslavia; his parents emigrated to the United States when he was still a young boy. His poetry, though written in American English, holds an atmosphere of Eastern European mystery and dread; in this, it resembles the folkloric surrealism of the Serbian poet Vasko Popa. As Simic has stated in an interview, "When I was young and just starting to write in English, Serbian words would often come into my mind and create difficulties.... English is the language that I know well and yet I speak it with an accent."

American (neo-)surrealist poetry also speaks with a foreign accent in the work of Edouard Roditi and Nanos Valaoritis. Both of these European-born writers have composed notable poetry in multiple languages, including English. Both poets have contributed regularly to American magazines and have had books published by American presses. Roditi was born in Paris in 1910 (and so belongs to the earliest generation of surrealist poets writing in English); as the son of an American citizen, he held U.S. citizenship, but attended schools in France and Britain, and first visited the U.S. in 1929. He claimed to have written the "first English and American surrealist manifesto" in 1929; entitled "The New Reality," it offers a brief restatement of a few themes from the first French manifesto. Many of Roditi's works take the form of the prose poem or prose fable; his style is characterized by a dry drollery, good old-fashioned grotesquery, and a somewhat leaden lyricism. Among his American publications are *Prose Poems: New Hieroglyphic Tales* (Kayak, 1968), *Emperor of Midnight* (Black Sparrow, 1974), and *Choose Your Own World* (Asylum Arts, 1992). Roditi died shortly after the last-mentioned book appeared.

Nanos Valaoritis shares Roditi's penchant for drollery, but in his case the inclination is more oblique, tilting the mind toward a glittering, many-eyed mystery. His poems typically play out a conceit as vast as it is absurd:

With great difficulty I manage to get out of my skin
After some hair-raising moments
        everything goes smoothly...
A quick tug is all it takes and I am out...
What an experience to see the world
Without the self's enveloping atmosphere
Everything is trembling with transparent colour
Women's thoughts are readable as the daily paper
The minds of little children contain untold marvels
The men magnificent like painted savages
The trees a patch of liquid green flowing
Into the earth's hands holding the sky's vessel...

In this poem, "The Birth of Second Sight," Valaoritis develops his comic premise inexorably toward a cosmic finale. His Borgesian conclusions are often profound, but his means of arriving at them are usually lighthearted: Valaoritis's strategy of estrangement has a twinkle in its eye that is both kindly and roguish; its expression is both bemused and amused. His inventiveness is splendidly exhibited in the prose poems collected in *My Afterlife Guaranteed* (City Lights, 1990): here are exercises in mise en abîme, presenting scenes that regress infinitely, as in "Borisofski's Lair" and "Progressive Distortion of 16th-Century Oil Painting"; the Freudian mythography of the "Edward Jaguar" stories; and Orientalist fabulations such as "Simoon" ("A vigilant eye flashes over the land like a searchlight.... Gliding over a dead donkey it illuminates a hole into which I am whispering my last secrets").

Born in 1921 in Switzerland to Greek parents (and to a literary lineage, for his great-grandfather was a highly celebrated Greek poet), Valaoritis studied law at the University of Athens and English literature at London University. He has twice been awarded the Greek national poetry prize. For some decades, he has resided alternately in Athens, Paris, and the San Francisco Bay Area (where he taught for many years at SF State University).[2] In addition to *My Afterlife Guaranteed*, three other books by Valaoritis have been published by small presses in the United States: *Hired Hieroglyphs* (Kayak, 1971); *Diplomatic Relations* (Kayak, 1972); and *Flash Bloom* (Wire Press, 1980).

Roditi and Valaoritis were regular contributors to *kayak*, inspiring the magazine with a breath of living European surrealism. Indeed, the magazine's atmosphere held an overly high concentration of Euro-surrealism, while the distinctly American surrealist innovations of Lamantia, Kaufman, and Cortez were nowhere in evidence (here, it is not a question of nationalism but of opening a space for cultural self-definition). There was, however, one exception to *kayak*'s Eurocentrism: the poetry of Ivan Argüelles, an important surrealist innovator with a Mexican-American background, whose work began to appear in the magazine during the seventies.

Argüelles was born in Minnesota in 1939, but spent his early childhood in Mexico City. The son of a Mexican father and an American mother, Argüelles was raised bilingually; he attended high school in Minnesota and went on to study classics at the University of Chicago and then library science at Vanderbilt. As a young poet in the late fifties and early sixties, he felt the influence of the Beats, but also immersed himself in the literature of the Romance languages and High Modernism. Upon graduation from Vanderbilt, Argüelles was hired as a cataloger at the New York Public Library. It was there, in the library's poetry collection, that Argüelles discovered the poets of the New York School. As he later wrote in an autobiographical essay entitled "Asi Es la Vida," "What was this idiom,

---

2   Jerry Estrin, a Language poet who died of cancer in 1993, was a student of Valaoritis in the seventies. Largely as a result of Valaoritis's influence, Estrin defined his own work at that time as surrealist; the first issues of *Vanishing Cab,* the magazine that Estrin edited, also were charged with surrealist work. Eventually Estrin was drawn away from surrealism by the rise of Language poetry in the eighties. However, one of Estrin's first volumes of poetry, *A Book of Gestures* (Sombre Reptiles, 1980) bears on its cover the photo of a meeting between Gertrude Stein and André Breton: the photo is emblematic of a state of suspension between surrealism and text-centered poetry.

this racy colloquial and yet often surreal mélange? I was still swinging with Dante and the troubadors.... And then there was the gateway to the French surrealists through Ashbery and O'Hara.... My mind was in flames, multiplying in all directions. ...Between Vallejo and Breton my brain began to sunflower."

Somewhat later, Argüelles became attracted to Hitchcock's kayak magazine: "Heavily surreal, intelligent, and with great graphics, ...I thought this was one of the places for my work." But the turning point came with his discovery of Lamantia's poetry. As Argüelles put it, "Lamantia's mad, Beat-tinged American idiom surrealism had a very strong impact on me. Both intellectual and uninhibited, this was the dose for me." While Argüelles's early writings were rooted in neo-Beat bohemianism and Chicano culture, by the late seventies he was developing his own, highly energetic genus (and genius) of surrealism. Two collections of his poems were published in quick succession: *Instamatic Reconditioning* (Damascus Road, 1978) and *The Invention of Spain* (Downtown Poets Co-op, 1978). The latter volume especially still shows the undiminished influence of García Lorca and Vallejo; in Argüelles's subsequent work, however, Lamantia's star steadily gains precedence—until it, too, is submerged within the gong-tormented sea of Argüelles's kinematic (and cinematic) encyclopedism.

In 1978, Argüelles moved to the West Coast to work as librarian at the University of California at Berkeley. Here, he encountered only a few other poets (including Nanos Valaoritis and the present writer) who shared his committment to surrealism. (Lamantia, who also resided in the Bay Area, had withdrawn into hermetic solitude and remained unresponsive to Argüelles's efforts to contact him.) By the early eighties, Argüelles was preparing a third collection of his poems; as he remarked in his memoir, "The poems I chose for this set exhibited a greater variety of topics and styles than the previous two books. The surrealism was more intense." This collection, entitled *Captive of the Vision of Paradise*, was published in a handsome edition in 1982 by Hartmus Press. The cover art, depicting the arrow-penetrated torso of

St. Sebastian, proved to be apt, for it introduced a predominant theme of Argüelles's mature period—namely, that of (often eroticized) mystical suffering.

> the ancient city swings like a leaf
> beneath the flaming prism
> I am captive here this side
> of the second hour never to reach
> the third and the sea with its castle
> of salt and the air with its dark
> how they take me and ride me
> through the day's ruthless onslaught!

From Lamantia, he inherited such stylistic trademarks as the frequent use of exclamation points and capitalization; but Argüelles is even more passionately predisposed than Lamantia to the use of dramatic rhetoric. Also, the scope of Argüelles's erudition, thanks to a multilingual talent encompassing everything from Sanskrit to Old Icelandic, is wider (if not wilder) than Lamantia's. Citations of world-historical places, texts, and personages proliferate throughout Argüelles's poems—their kaleidoscopic facets always reflecting the central fact of the poet's anguish.

By the time he relocated to the West Coast, Argüelles had mastered an "automatic" mode of writing that allowed him to produce prodigious quantities of poems, which stormed and swarmed their way through the small-press literary landscape of the eighties. (In a survey of "most frequently published poets" conducted by the International Directory of Small-Press Publishers in 1988, Argüelles was ranked fourth.) At the same time, Argüelles's style continued to evolve: his poetic line was lengthening and loosening, his emotional content was deepening and darkening, and his imagery was becoming an increasingly turbulent montage that now derived many of its elements from popular culture and current events. For example, on the occasion of the explosion of the space shuttle Challenger in 1986, Argüelles penned the poem entitled "Autoincineration of the Right Stuff": "we suffer these things imagining swiftly the immediate demise of the imagination / take my fingers off feed them to the impossible fish of URANUS / I hear their music their moons their clouds of insane love / THE MASTERGUIDE IS NO MORE IN THE NAME OF YAHWEH APOLLO AKHNATON / the supreme eye burns itself just as the numinous mouth devours itself / jazz cycles of infinity repeated on eternal screen Dan Rather / who will count the children? who will walk the dog? where are we? / suddenly air is impact the heaviest thing we can ever know."

In the late eighties, Argüelles finally encountered Lamantia at a reading the latter was giving in Berkeley. Argüelles recollected the incident in his memoir: "For years I had assiduously been sending him my books and chapbooks, without any response to speak of. I was pleased that he enjoyed my company as much as he did when we finally met." Argüelles had just written a laudatory review of Lamantia's *Meadowlark West*, contrasting the "holism" of the new book with the "demonism" of Lamantia's earlier collection, *Destroyed Works*. According to Argüelles, Lamantia deemed the review, which appeared in the October 1986 issue of *Poetry Flash*, to be "perfect." But Argüelles's contact with Lamantia was fleeting and ultimately unsatisfying: "A difficult person, with dogmatic tendencies, Philip struck up a brief friendship with me," Argüelles wrote in his memoir. "But I felt he wanted a disciple, ...and not an equal, as a companion."

Aside from a scattering of staple-bound chapbooks, no further volumes of Argüelles's poetry appeared until 1989. (In general, the publication of books of American surrealist poetry declined in the eighties. While many factors can be correlated with this decline—the political counter-revolution of Reaganism, economic stagnation, the academization of avant-garde culture—its major cause was undoubtedly the extinction of a certain kind of imaginal fire. Surrealism in the post-Vietnam era, as in the post-WWII era, was perceived to have exhausted itself. Perhaps the situation is best delineated in the form

ANDREW JORON

of a question: To what extent did the defeat of the radical social as-
pirations of the sixties and early seventies entail the rejection, among
the American avant-garde, of a poetics of the imagination?) At this
time, Argüelles, still a tiger burning bright, assembled a collection
of hard-edged, streetwise poems into his biggest book yet (169 pages
long), entitled *Looking for Mary Lou: Illegal Syntax.* This project
was a collaboration with photographer Craig Stockfleth, whose visu-
als (Romantic-realist studies in black-and-white) are displayed on the
book's left-hand pages; Argüelles's poems appear on the right. Next to
the coolness of the photographs, the poems rage like a conflagration or
a ritual destruction: "smoking black combustion of invisible fish fried
against their own hieroglyphs / steaming absences of the universe how
she revives at the end of the hour / graced on either lip with the tat-
toes of the muses whose lipstick is DEATH."

In this book, as in most of his subsequent work, the poet's despair
more and more assumes a mythically feminine shape: an anima-fig-
ure who functions as the embodiment of an eroticized death wish.
Different names, such as Mary Lou or Persephone or Madonna, are
attached to this figure, yet it is obvious that they are all manifestions
of the same fleur du mal. In later compositions, these symbols of the
poet's longing for (and simultaneous dread of) orgasmic annihilation
are subsumed under the horrific honorific "'That' Goddess."

Looking for Mary Lou: Illegal Syntax was chosen to receive the
1989 William Carlos Williams Award of the Poetry Society of
America. Empowered by this unexpected recognition, Argüelles
immediately set out to produce an epic poem comprised of multiple books, with the overarching title *Pantograph.* As he reports in
his autobiography, "I wrote [the first volume] "That" Goddess" in
a white heat of two months (106 pages between February 10 and
April 25, 1990)." As a book-length surrealist poem in English,
"That" Goddess is unprecedented—the only comparable achieve-
ments are, in Spanish, Huidobro's *Altazor* and, in French, *Tzara's
L'homme approximatif.* It is "a deafening reportage from the other

world, the one we are always / skirting, careful lest we fall into Persephone's infernal / but gorgeous embrace, when not even a sequence of connected / thoughts is of any avail, yes 'that' goddess, or Arachne / or Ariadne...." The tonality of the poem is subject to manic mood-swings, racing up and down the scales between between tragic lamentation and triumphant declamation, with plenty of blackly humorous asides and Sadean eroticism along the way. Keith Tuma, reviewing the book in Sulfur, observed that "Argüelles plugs his unabashedly confused and lucid meditations and exhortations concerning women, myth, and culture into a loose adaptation of Virgilian epic. The book is one vast catalogue of the abjection, misogyny, lust, and ego-stroking that is manhood as the modernists mostly understood it, turning about the specter of the indescribable unapproachable woman smoking a cigarette in the banal pose of the femme fatal." The point can be made even more emphatically: the first volume of *Pantograph* is a neo-surrealist testimonial to the poet's devotion to the Muse as Dominatrix.

Another poet who rose to prominence in the pages of kayak and has since become an important representative of West Coast neo-surrealism is the British expatriate Adam Cornford. Eleven years younger than Argüelles, Cornford arrived in the U.S. in 1969, enrolling at the University of California at Santa Cruz. There, he attended George Hitchcock's writing workshop and fell under the spell of the neo-surrealist synthesis that Hitchcock was forging between American imagism and European surrealism. Some of Cornford's workshop poems in this style were selected by Hitchcock to appear in *kayak*. Cornford came to regard Hitchcock as a mentor; he briefly served as assistant to the editor, helping to sift through unsolicited submissions. At the same time, Cornford was also discovering the original texts of surrealism, studying Breton's manifestos and translating poems by Eluard and Péret.

In 1973, Cornford entered the graduate writing program at San Francisco State University. Here, he flourished under the kindly tutelage of the Greek surrealist Nanos Valaoritis. Although he also regarded Valaoritis as a mentor, Cornford had passed beyond the phase of imitation that was evident in his work under Hitchcock. In the twilight of the radical movements of the sixties, Cornford set himself the task of creating a politically engaged form of poetry combining the energies of surrealism and situationism. As he stated in an autobiographical essay, "I wanted to use the 'convulsive' image developed by surrealism in a more deliberate, targeted way, so as to bypass people's conditioned numbness and renew and clarify their awareness of their social situation."

> Cold word evaporating off the lips
> the television says it is something enormous
> a skyscraper with glass bones
> a priest tells us it has always been
> because God holds all the keys to our eyes. . .

In the same spirit, Cornford participated in—and shared a Berkeley residence with—a post-situationist political groupuscule during this period. Another member of the household was the fine-arts printer Peter Koch, who expressed an interest in Cornford's poetry. Within a year, Koch had returned to his native Montana, where he launched *Montana Gothic*, a magazine whose form ("rude" typography and collages) and content (imagism and surrealism) showed the strong influence of Hitchcock's *kayak*. (Six issues were published between 1974 and 1977, featuring poems by Cornford, Valaoritis, and Hitchcock, among many others.) In conjunction with the magazine, Koch also founded Black Stone Press, and offered to publish Cornford's first poetry collection. In 1978, *Shooting Scripts* was printed in Missoula, Montana, in a fine letter-press edition illustrated by the Chilean collagist Ludwig Zeller. As the book's title indicates, visual imagery is paramount in Cornford's poetics: almost every poem presented here, whether political or lyrical or both, is predicated on the visual manifestation of the marvellous. But Cornford's language is not simply a "mirror of the marvellous," passively receiving signals from beyond. Instead, Cornford's language itself produces the marvellous by means of a highly structured machinery of visual metaphor. In the loom of his language, metaphors are interlaced and lengthened to make a colorful textile—a textured text—whose exfoliating patterns repeat the invisible ideality of a master pattern or conceit. In "Shootout at Cranium Gulch," for example, the conceit (inspired by a line from Lautréamont) interweaves a narrative genre, the Western, with an existentialist theology:

> God's reflection grins at him with aurora teeth.
> He draws and fires. Bottles shatter,
> but God hops aside
> like a magnified flea, and out through the swingdoors.
> On the street lined with flickers
> God faces him, a stampede suddenly frozen.
> He fires again. God's blood splashes
> and napalms a horse into screaming anatomy.
> The man in the cobra-skin squeezes the trigger
> until his gun is empty.
> Then God fires, spread out like a continent.
> Bullets pass through the man's bones
> with the speed of cosmic rays.
> Smiling, he understands. . .
> The thin dark man watches God
> gallop slowly away into the vanishing-point
> at the center of his head. . .

Here, the state of surreality no longer possesses the "naturalistic" immediacy of a dream or an act of free association. Instead, it first must be mediated—or made visible—by a formal structure. Paradoxically, the imagination is liberated, not by loosening the constraints on expression, but by binding the elements of language together in a new way (otherwise stated: the theory and practice of neo-surrealist metaphor requires something like a theory of knots).

In 1987, Cornford became director of the Poetics Program at New College in San Francisco. In the following year, a new collection of his poems, entitled Animations, was published by City Lights. Nearly half of this collection is taken up by a single poem, "Lightning-Rod to Storm." The poem's vast conceit maps the quarrel of a pair of lovers onto the discharge of energy between a lightning–rod and an electrical storm. "All this / Has been a means of travelling far and fast, of lifting the instruments / Of a viewpoint above dirty weather that / Was both of us." "Lightning-Rod to Storm" is Cornford's masterpiece: more than an exercise in extended metaphor, it is a dazzling display of analogical consciousness that, like the speculative cosmologies of the Renaissance, follows a thread of resemblances through the labyrinth of space and time. Moreover, these resemblances (as in the writings of Giordano Bruno and other Renaissance magi) are frequently derived from science and technology:

> ...anti-star whose deep gravity
> Ghosts and streams all the sights of the world inward
> Into a momentary virtual image, a dazzle-hologram
> Of elsewhere,
> there at the event horizon—

Cornford's imagery progresses futureward, through scenes of social revolution, along a continuum from actual to potential, "shift[ing] the invisible into the spectrum not only / Of knowledge, but of astonishment." This, of course, is the trajectory of utopian narrative and of science fiction—indeed, several other poems in Animations are even more explicit in their use of science-fictional tropes.

Such tropes have assumed an even greater prominence in Cornford's subsequent work. His longest poem yet, "The Snarling Gift" (which appears in *Terminal Velocities*, an anthology published by Pantograph Press in 1993), narrates the emergence of a "kind of intelligent sub-program manifested by the Earth itself as a response to ecological degradation." This salvational "sub-program" comes to inhabit the mind and body of a Chicana nurse caught up in a social revolution of the future. "The Snarling Gift" once again exhibits Cornford's talent for expanding and contracting a metaphorical conceit through a multitude of referential frames (in accordance, perhaps, with the diastolic and systolic pulsations of Blake's Eternity).

> She [the Snarling Gift] emerges
> In the sunken vault of the thalamus, cable-jungle
> Where the senses converge.
> 　　　　Her own vestigial image
> Sweeps past her, gigantic ghost-mask on its way
> To be understood.

The style of the "The Snarling Gift" is as protean as its main character, shifting from social realism to mythic fantasy. The text is also typographically complex, verging at times on concrete or "pattern" poetry. These experiments in typography foreshadow the diagrammatic format of "The Cyborg's Path," a series of science-fiction poems that Cornford began in the nineties. The decidedly "speculative" turn of Cornford's recent work is evident in his third collection, *Decision Forest* (published in 1997 by Pantograph Press), which contains several poems from the "Cyborg's Path" sequence as well as "Millennium: A Topology," a cycle of densely-worded science-fiction poems.

There are obvious affinities between the traditions of surrealism and science fiction. They are descended from a common ancestor—the literature of visionary Romanticism—and they share its aspiration toward the astonishing revelation of otherness. Both surrealism and science fiction acquired definitive form in the twenties; yet, for most of their histories, they have evolved along parallel paths. In the sixties, however, their paths began to converge, both in the paintings of Matta and in so-called New Wave science fiction (especially in the work of J.G. Ballard and Brian Aldiss). Efforts by poets to synthesize the two forms were made sporadically (and more or less independently) until the mid seventies, when a community of "speculative" poets began to take shape around a core of publications (such as *Speculative Poetry Review* edited by Robert Frazier). In 1982, the present writer launched a magazine of speculative poetry, *Velocities*, dedicated to "traversing the space between science fiction and surrealism." The magazine, whose fifth and final issue appeared in 1988, was fashioned after the model of kayak and featured contributors such as Valaoritis, Argüelles, and Cornford. Within this rather recondite milieu of "neo-surrealist science-fiction poetry," some single-author collections were also produced: *All the Clocks Are Melting* by Bruce Boston (Velocities, 1984); *Science Fiction* (Pantograph, 1992) by the present writer; and *Dream Protocols* (Talisman of Indiana, 1992) and *Phase Language* (Pantograph, 1995) by Lee Ballentine. Several anthologies also have been issued in this sub-genre, including *Poly: New Speculative Writing*, edited by Lee Ballentine (Ocean View, 1989) and *Burning with a Vision*, edited by Robert Frazier (Owlswick, 1984). At a time when when most American avant-garde poetry was preoccupied with its own textuality, these speculative poets (unabashed heirs of Romanticism) sought a visionary opening in the experience of technological society—prefiguring, as in Cornford's millenial topology, the mind of a "mutant whose passions are to ours as a Bud Powell solo is to a door chime."

In the mid to late nineties, the San Francisco poet John Nòto promoted a "new synthesis" of cyberpunk, surrealism, and postmodern poetry. In 1997, he launched the magazine *Orpheus Grid* and co-founded, with the poet David Hoefer, *Vatic Hum Press*. By the turn of the millennium, both magazine and press had ceased operations; nonetheless, the project remains noteworthy for its attempt to reformat surrealism as a kind of "digital delirium." The texts of Nòto's *Psycho-motor Breathscapes* and Hoefer's *New, Improved Wilderness* (both published by Vatic Hum in

1997) are crowded with the dreamlike juxtapositions caused by information overload. Lindsay Hill's NdjenFerno, published by *Vatic Hum* in 1998, is a poetic upgrade of Anthony Burgess's *Clockwork Orange*, with its near-future lingo of ultraviolence.

The resonances between surrealism and various genres of high and low fantasy (including the fairy tale) also have been picked up and amplified by certain American poets. In the early eighties, Detroit poet and artist Thomas Wiloch published and edited Grimoire, a magazine devoted to surrealist fantasy; it featured colored paper in the tradition of kayak as well as unusually skillful collages by the editor himself. Wiloch has written a book of prose poems, Mr. Templeton's *Toyshop* (Jazz Police Books, 1995), that hauntingly harmonizes surrealism and the modern genre of "dark" fantasy. Beat scholar Stephen Ronan's chapbook *Nights of October* (Ammunition Press, 1985) is a sequence of Halloween-flavored poems "concerned with Philip Lamantia and derived from conversations with him." And Christina Zawadiwsky's *The Hand on the Head of Lazarus* (Ion Books, 1986) is a convulsively beautiful collection of neo-surrealist poems and prose poems redolent with the violence and sensuality of Eastern European folklore (the author, born in New York and now a resident of Milwaukee, is of Ukrainian descent).

Folktales and fairy tales have traditionally functioned as zones of "permissible transgression," as cultural reservoirs of collectively shared illicit desires. This spirit of transgression is well captured in the work of Rikki Ducornet. Born in New York in 1943 and now residing in Denver (after long stays in France and South America), Ducornet has written six volumes of poems—most memorably *Weird Sisters* (Intermedia, 1976) and *Knife Notebook* (Fiddlehead, 1977)—whose vivid and visceral neo-surrealist imagery seems to be drawn from some well of legend. Her style has been described by the critic J. H. Matthews as "an unsettling mixture of monstrosity and humor, for which the closest parallel—in surrealism or anywhere outside—is to be found in the prose and verse of Joyce Mansour."

Such amalgamations of surrealism with other literary traditions might be considered as late, decadent chimerae or as minor offshoots from the main body of the movement. But the development of neo-surrealism in the United States resembles a fractal pattern whose mode of generation is nonlinear, and whose various elements stand in a nonhierarchical relation to one another. The sudden, spontaneous apparition of the sun through the night-meshes of conventionalized discourse cannot be foretold from within that discourse.

Among the most unprecedented and fiery of all such apparitions is the work of Will Alexander. As Alexander testifies, "It is not with the steepness of vultures that I seek to procure an arcane stability in the void, but by the blending of halts and motions, like the vertical equilibria of fire, brought to an incandescent pitch of value." (He is speaking here in the voice of "The Whirling King in the Runic Psychic Theatre.") Alexander's work participates in, but can hardly be confined to, the pan-African surrealist tradition of Cortez and Césaire. The explosion of his language engulfs almost every continent and sweeps away the categories that separate poetry and philosophy, myth and science. Three collections of Alexander's poetry have been released: *Vertical Rainbow Climber* (Jazz Press, 1987); *Asia & Haiti* (Sun & Moon, 1995); and *The Stratospheric Canticles* (Pantograph Press, 1995). He is also the author of a book of essays, *Towards the Primeval Lightning Field* (O Books, 1998). Each book is illustrated by the visual force-fields of Alexander's own artwork.

Will Alexander was born (in 1948) and raised in Los Angeles and attended UCLA. He alludes to a painful process of self-education in his first book: "Outside myself and bleeding on my own discoveries I discover in a cave Pythagorean lodestones broken in the air of Chaldean snake myths." During those years of self-discovery, Alexander worked mostly in isolation, becoming the conduit for a primal and oracular speech. His surrealism has most often been compared to that of Césaire. The comparison is not inaccurate; yet Césaire's language, while similarly energetic, is thoroughly dialogical (as if he were facing a circle of auditors) whereas Alexander's is monological (as if he were orbiting the earth).

Moreover, as Garrett Caples has pointed out, "Alexander's surrealism is not about 'the image' but about 'the word.'" Obviously, Alexander's self-fashioning as a poet did not start from that centralizing point of view demanded by scopic discourse. Instead, he positioned himself within the contingent order of the lexicon, refashioning (and thus reclaiming) language word by word. As a result, Alexander's writing liberates the imagination from the restricted economy of the image:

> though shattered by various Saxon devices
> I am the flame throughout the soaring absolute
> I denigrate
> I take on sanguine territorial opposition
> with a force
> enriched
> with untoward fertility
> with a dominate tendency to waver
> with excessive a-regional metrics
> with inhaled phantasmatics
> spilled on fortuitous migrational soils
> there is ermine
> there is discourse by nugget
> there is scarification by increase

As is evident in these lines from *The Stratospheric Canticles*' "Song in Barbarous Fumarole of the Japanese Crested Ibis," the linguistic turn of Alexander's practice melts metaphor and metonymy together to make a new glyph of meaning. This Alexandrian glyph is typically formed by neologisms and etymological dislocations; by "focus throws" between denotation and connotation; and by the radical recontextualization of specialized vocabularies.

Caples insightfully comments that "Alexander's privileging of the word as medium in poetry no doubt partially accounts for his penchant for the dramatic monologue." But Alexander's monologues rarely communicate the experience of an atomized individual speaker; rather, the monological voice is unified and legitimized only by relaying signals from elsewhere, from some transindividual level of being. The two long poems collected in *Asia & Haiti* are composed in the plural voice. In "Asia," it is "a collective voice of rebellious Buddhist monks who hover in invisibility, vertically exiled, in an impalpable spheroid, virescently tinged, subtly flecked with scarlet, conducting astral warfare against the Chinese invasion and occupation of Tibet." In "Haiti," the voice is that of les Morts, the dead souls of the Duvalier dictatorship's victims. In both poems, the tone is appropriately accusatory; here, however, the crimes of the oppressors are judged, not according to conventional legal or moral standards, but "with the seismic zeal of darkened speculation." Alexander hurls down his glyphic phrases as weapons, as instruments of revendication, for they contain the power of the Word's poetic autonomy. Thus, Alexander's voice, with its glyphic revaluation of received meanings, is as much autonomist as automatist—a voice that, in giving its own law to itself, naturally takes the form of a (collective) monologue.

At the same time, it is apparent that Alexander does not wish to simply cancel the received meaning of a given word in order to replace it with his own meaning. Each of Alexander's books comes with a glossary in which the origin and interrelation of certain words is explained. This practice has evoked the ire of literary critic Mark Scroggins, who, in a review of *Asia & Haiti*, complained that "the careful annotation of exoticisms and their seemingly arbitrary deployment within the poem work at cross purposes to one another." While this complaint is misguided, Scroggins nonetheless makes a key observation: in Alexander's practice, the meaning of the same word is simultaneously defined and indefinite, setting a vivid dialectic of freedom and determinism in motion within the poem's linguistic order.

Once caught up in this dialectic, words no longer can be expected to serve a strictly referential function, or even an allusive one. Along with the significative aspect of words, their purely material aspect as shapes and sounds enters into play in the poem. Words thereby acquire some of the qualities of paint in the works of those surrealist artists who stand on the cusp of abstract expressionism, such as Gorky and Matta. In such artworks, the paint thickens and clots at strategic nodes into a three-dimensional object, then thins and slides away to become a representational medium, playing surface textures against perspectival depth. What Scroggins perceives as "cross purposes" in Alexander's writing are actually kinetic interactions between referential and non-referential planes, an important feature of the poet's painterly style. But there is a political corollary to be drawn as well: these interactions tend to resist the encirclement of the imagination by authoritarian forms of discourse. The poet's ability to liberate language in this way is a magic weapon, and part of the spell he is casting against oppression in Asia and Haiti.

Besides poetry, Alexander has written novels, short stories, and plays. In all of these forms, Alexander allows the autonomous Word to come into being in its own way: either to drop vertiginously into a semiotic space of unexpected correspondences or to become a merely localized fillip of sonic or graphic texture. Under the terms of this allowance, the Word, prior to its emergence, is recognized to exist in a state akin to nothingness, yet charged with potential. Thus, there are frequent invocations to the awaited Word's vertical, vortical, tornado-like suspension. For example, in his play, *Conduction in the Catacombs* (published in Hambone no. 13 [1997]), the "bodiless vortex" is divided "through the corporeal" into two characters in a sanatorium setting, where "the authorities have no other cause than having us eat ourselves alive in a mirror." This enforced mirroring or self-division has tragic consequences; nonetheless, as one character admits, "we take from brokenness a message or a hawk, across scattered lamps and trees. It is the necessary ritual." And the other responds, "The Elysium!"

Alexander's prioritization of the "word" rather than the "image" initiates, as stated above, a linguistic turn within neo-surrealist practice. This turn is convergent with the emergence, in post-sixties American experimental poetry, of the Language school. This new group of experimentalists regarded the sixties' poetics of the expressive imagination as a failed utopia. Rather than a poetics of enthusiasm, a poetics of skepticism was advocated: the Romanticism of the metaphoric image was rejected in favor of the "realism" of the metonymic cut-up. Members of the Language movement presented a forceful, sometimes militant, program that resituated the literary techniques of disjunction and recontextualization—as developed by Stein, Zukofsky, and Olson—within a critical theory of the "social text" then current among the academic left.

From the start, the Language poets were careful to distinguish their practice from that of surrealism. One of the movement's chief theoreticians, Barrett Watten, in an essay on "Method and Surrealism," criticized the valorization of the "private image" and the "identity of perception and representation" in Breton's work; in another essay, Watten compared a passage from Breton's "Soluble Fish" to texts by Carla Harryman and Kit Robinson, concluding that the latter's work demonstrated "not the coming into being of the image but of something even deeper—the perception of the mind in control of its language. Distance, rather than absorption, is the intended effect." Undeterred by these demarcations, a few poets and critics have sought to investigate the pre-existing affinities, as well as the potential for collaboration, between the two movements.

Charles Borkhuis, in an essay written in 1991, stated that "this gap between Late Surrealism and Textual (including 'Language') poetry may prove to be a magnetically charged, yet largely unexplored area." In this important essay ("Late Surrealism and American 'Language' Poetry," published in Onthebus no. 8/9), Borkhuis argued that "both Surrealism and 'Language' poetry are attempts to decenter the idea of the self-as-creator"; in both forms, "the text is read as an accumulation of poetic evidence" rather than as the testament of "a particular ego." In light of the work of writers such as Michael Palmer and John Yau, whose texts are "open-ended and dispersed throughout the body," Borkhuis envisioned a form of "Parasurrealist/Textual" practice, where "thought is not outside, observing this process [of writing], but part of it; it finds itself in-situation."

The poetry of John Yau has increasingly become both surrealist and serialist: in his latest collection, *Forbidden Entries* (Black Sparrow, 1996), permutations of words intermingle with and motivate patterns of self-distancing imagery. For example, the poem "Angel Atrapado XXIII," the line "A torn sheet hovering above an empty yield" is rescued from pastoral surrealism by the substitition of a single letter. By writing "yield," and thus forcing a detour in the line's own drive toward the word "field," Yau, with an elegant gesture, incites a struggle between the material text and its imaginal content. This maneuver, which is replicated throughout Yau's recent work, permits the (sometimes agonistic) embrace of self-reflexive textuality and surrealist imagery: "This tongue is a flower. Someday you will hear what it has to pay."

The struggle between the sign and the seen in Yau's writing is also played out on the thematic level of self-identity. In the many passages where self and other are constructed as a series of morphing masks, the poem becomes a palimpsest of textual skepticism and imagistic enthusiasm: "I was the toad in tinsel, / you were the donkey in red suede." The effect of such imagery is distancing rather than absorptive. In *Forbidden Entries* and his previous collection, Edificio Sayonara (Black Sparrow, 1992), Yau seems to be drafting documents of ecstatic doubt.

Occasionally, Yau's earlier work—which can be surveyed in a volume of selected poems, *Radiant Silhouette* (Black Sparrow, 1989)—also stages an encounter between serialism and surrealism (for example, the imagery of "Broken Off by the Music" relies on the recombinant splicing of textual fragments). For the most part, the surrealism of *The Sleepless Night of Eugene Delacroix* (1980) and *Broken Off by the Music* (1981) stands closer to that of Ashbery and O'Hara. By the time *Corpse and Mirror* was published in 1983, however, Yau had magnified the New

York school's surrealizing tendencies considerably. And by the time of *Dragon's Blood* (1989), Yau had turned the Russian futurists' "baring of the device" (a strategy reclaimed by the Language poets) into a surrealist act: "When the last mirage / evaporates, I will be / the sole proprietor of this voice / and all its rusted machinery."

Within the Language and post-Language writing community, several poets have begun to explore the "magnetically charged" gap between surrealism and textual poetry first indicated by Borkhuis in 1991. One of those poets is Borkhuis himself, whose poem-cycle *Hypnogogic Sonnets* (Red Dust, 1992) thematizes the body as half writing surface, half dream-object. In his later collections *Proximity* (Stolen Arrows) (Sink, 1994) and *Alpha Ruins* (Bucknell University Press, 1999), the condition of textuality itself serves as a generator of images: "letters pulsing / radiant foliage behind thought- / splinters that break / the skin...." Similarly, my book of surrational poems, *The Removes* (Hard Press, 1999), embraces language as a paradoxical body.

The poems of Phillip Foss, too, transform the text into a palpable body by means of inventive typographic realignments, spatializations of meaning that are at once speculative and sensual. In "The Elegant Predations," Foss professes the "intent... to create a church of sound, a baroque vehicle for image, and these a sonata of bastard symbols." Foss's work enacts a neo-surrealist invocation to otherness within the framework of self-reflexive textuality. His collections include *The Composition of Glass* (Lost Roads, 1988), *The Excesses the Caprices* (Light and Dust, 1991), and *Courtesan of Seizure* (Light and Dust, 1993). Among other post-Language poets working in this "magnetically charged gap" are John Olson, W. B. Keckler, Kristin Prevallet (especially in her homage to Max Ernst, *Perturbation, My Sister* [Leave Books, 1994]), Jeff Clark, Brian Lucas, and Garrett Caples.

The history of neo-surrealism in American poetry is not a linear story whose future is determined by its past. It is a sleepwalker armed with reason. As such, it arrives both too late and too early: a solar apparition at midnight.

AFTERWORD

Ten years have passed since the original publication of this essay in the anthology *The World in Time and Space* edited by Edward Foster and Joseph Donahue. The aim of that anthology was to provide an overview of American poetry and poetics in the latter half of the twentieth century. As a chapter in this anthology, my contribution was necessarily limited both in its scope and its length: I could discuss the works of only those poets with a declared affinity to surrealism who had, moreover, published at least one book before the century's end.

The essay was expanded slightly on the occasion of its publication as a chapbook for Black Square Editions in 2004. Nonetheless, in that edition as well as the present one, many poets whose work is influenced by surrealism were left out of consideration simply because of the limited space imposed by the chapbook format. A comprehensive study of American surrealist poetry demands a lengthy monograph to do it justice, and I hope one will be forthcoming.

Looking back at the last ten years, one finds that the influence of surrealism has hardly abated; it may even have increased somewhat due to the proliferation of reprints of classical surrealist texts and the equally proliferating academic studies of these texts. Given the academicization of American poetry in general, this recent infusion of surrealist discourse throughout the humanities curriculum can't fail to have some effect on the practice of writing-school graduates. However, the imitation of surrealism is not surrealism; in the phrase of André Breton, surrealism is elsewhere.

At the same time, prolonged exposure to the works of classical surrealism may yield unexpected results. The shock-effect of an encounter with de Chirico's painting profoundly changed the life of Yves Tanguy, for example (admittedly, this encounter did not occur within an institutional setting). Still, because surrealism refuses to be stabilized as a self-consistent body of doctrine, consisting only in a beautifully convulsive act, there is no way to understand and to practice "surrealism" without transforming it. In other words, surrealism must exceed itself in order to remain surrealism. The desire that exceeds any possible object races through—even as it erases—the object-world along a nonlinear and unpredictable lightning-path. Such absolute desire provokes a "crisis of the object" (in the words of Breton once again), indicating that surrealist provocation takes place at an ontological level that exceeds the human sphere itself.

Amid signs—which have increased exponentially in the past ten years—that capitalist civilization is arriving at its endgame, there is no need to argue for the ongoing relevance of the surrealist project. Postmodernism's ironic deconstruction of the commodity is at best a critical moment (one that was already anticipated and sublated by surrealism at its inception), which, if another world is possible, must be augmented by a creative moment driven not by commodity-logic but by the free association of the producers.

ANDREW JORON

Of course, a surrealist poem can't change the world. But a cry of protest, in such confluence that revolutionary action becomes inevitable, will change the world. The genius of surrealism has been to discover that the cry of protest is also an act of imagination, and to insist that precisely that imagination is more powerful than reality. The cry is a crack in the world, revealing what lies beyond.

It is this sense of something beyond the circulation of signs and commodities that is missing in contemporary poetry. However, what surrealism offers—what surrealism demands—is not a relapse into belief in a transcendent Beyond, but a visionary materialism that is alert and alive to the ways that reality itself is liable to boil over (starting with the "profane illumination" that Benjamin recognized in surrealist practice).

At the end of the first decade of the twenty-first century, perhaps it is time to announce again, as Breton did in the Second Manifesto of 1930, "THE OCCULTATION OF SURREALISM." An occulted surrealist practice certainly runs through the dominant trend in American avant-garde poetry today—namely in the synthesis of Language writing and the New York School. Whereas the influence of surrealism on the latter is very well documented, the case for Language writing's debt to surrealism is only beginning to be argued by scholars such as David Arnold, whose *Poetry and Language Writing: Objective and Surreal* was published in 2007.[1]

The American poet most devoted to the occultation of surrealism—as a literal turn toward the occult, toward a gnosis subversive of capitalist reason—was Philip Lamantia, who passed away in 2005 at the age of 77. Lamantia's death marks the end of an era in American surrealist poetry, i.e. the era that carried the first wave of surrealism into the United

---

1   Of course, Breton was calling in the Second Manifesto for a *deliberate* occulation of surrealism, and for a surrealist swerve into the occult sciences, in order to prevent it from becoming reified and calcified as a mere "art movement." Similarly, the reinvention of surrealism in the twenty-first century will necessitate an *unlearning* of many notions that have accrued to the term "surrealism."

States. (Among Lamantia's cohorts in this first wave can be counted Charles Henri Ford, Parker Tyler, and—as David Arnold's book makes clear—William Carlos Williams.) Lamantia's inward-turning hermeticism made of surrealism an almost secret practice, restricted to a circle of initiates; nevertheless, he broadcast the surrealist Word widely by his example. Lamantia is considered by many to be the greatest American surrealist poet; without doubt, the landscape of the twenty-first century will continue to be haunted by his presence.

The second wave of surrealist writing in the U.S. broke and bifurcated, during the fifties and sixties, into various channels represented by the New York School, Deep Image, and the orthodox Chicago School, led by Franklin and Penelope Rosemont. The adherents of the Chicago School denounced the "revisionism" of other offshoots of surrealism, refusing to participate in the literary scene at large and placing militant political action at the forefront of surrealist practice.[2] As part of this program, the Chicago School sought to identify surrealist elements in American folk and working-class culture, especially the blues. To further their commitment to public agitation, the Chicago School's Black Swan Press has published scores of surrealist books and pamphlets, as well as the magazine *Arsenal.* With the death of Franklin Rosemont in 2009, yet another pillar of American surrealism has toppled.

The deaths of Lamantia and Rosemont mean that, at the outset of the twenty-first century, American surrealism has lost, respectively, its esoteric and exoteric faces. What face will surrealism now wear? Answer: surrealism will always show the face of the Sun at night.

---

2   The work of Laurence Weisberg, while falling within the strictures of classical surrealism, is possessed of a grace and depth that is often missing in the strident automatism of the Chicago School. However, like the members of the Chicago School, Weisberg never submitted his work for publication outside the surrealist circle. And he remained a fugitive presence even within this circle, as he struggled with the alcohol and drug addiction that eventually led to his early demise in 2003. A collection of his poems, simply entitled *Poems,* was privately issued in 2004.

As such, its face will flare unexpectedly, out of joint with time and space. For example, a major American poet, a member of that literary scene despised by orthodox surrealists, announced herself—quite late in her life—to be a surrealist poet. That poet was Barbara Guest. When Guest declared, at a lecture given at a New York gallery in the mid-eighties, "I grew up under the shadow of surrealism," she inaugurated the most productive and deeply original period in her work extending from the publication of *Fair Realism* in 1989 to her final collection, *The Red Gaze*, in 2005. Residing in New York in the fifties, Guest had watched surrealist painting develop into abstract expressionism in the work of such artists as Gorky and Motherwell. And in view of her New York School connections, Guest's poetry is often interpreted in terms of abstract expressionist art. Yet I believe the influence on Guest of not only surrealist art and but also surrealist literature—with its valorization of the gothic—proved to be more lasting. For it was a decidedly gothic version of neo-surrealism that Guest articulated in the late twentieth and early twenty-first centuries, as evidenced in such poems as "Dissonance Royal Traveller." Shortly before Guest passed away in 2006, at a conference given in her honor at the Berkeley Art Museum, she reaffirmed that "I have become a surrealist poet," adding, "Better late than never."

The surrealist influence in American avant-garde poetry is pervasive; yet among well-known poets whose work shows obvious affinities to surrealism (one could name John Ashbery, Michael Palmer, Clayton Eshleman, for starters), none has declared their surrealist identity as strongly as Guest in her last years. The full story will have to be told elsewhere, but at least a brief mention must be made here of several poets now rising to prominence whose work proceeds directly from an engagement with surrealism.

Two of these poets—John Olson and George Kalamaras—have been actively engaged with surrealism throughout their careers, but neither had published full-length collections by the end of the last century, so were left out of consideration in my original essay. In addition to writing poetry, Kalamaras has done primary research on world-historical surrealism, going far beyond the movement's origins in France to explore the work of poets practicing as surrealists in Japan, Greece, and Eastern Europe. See, for example, his article on the Japanese surrealist poet Takiguchi Shuzo, "The Air Is a Beautiful Princess Without Bones," in *Factorial 5* (2006). Kalamaras's own poetry rings with the newly-invented rituals of a global village, electrified by uncanny connectivities that are liable to remix language even at the level of syntax, as demonstrated by the title of his second collection *Borders My Bent Toward* (2003). A painting by the Mexican surrealist Remedios Varo, *The Creation of the Birds*, appears on the cover of the book: Varo's magical lyricism provides a highly appropriate visual counterpart to Kalamaras's writing. In "Could but Sound," the poet memorializes Varo's painting: "Great violins of electric moonlight string me down / so that I am bird, wings of a paraph." I am shocked by the charge of affirmation that runs through Kalamaras's work: "he looked down at his hand / it held hundreds of human eyes." Kalamaras has published four book-length collections of poetry in the past decade.

A different, but equally affirmative charge is felt in the poetry of John Olson, who practices a kind of "equipollent" writing in which words seem to explode out of each other. In a poem entitled "Trembling Gobbets of Language," Olson asks "How do you sew a pound / of accretion to the sound / of a needle of a noun? Thread it with a string / of explosions, Balinese // puppets & the collateral / of a throat clicking out of the lung / of an emotion // made of rain." Olson's writing appears to be attached to a secret dynamo at the heart of the wor(l)d, spinning and sputtering without stop. In his "Lament for Lamantia," Olson writes, "Surrealism is not word play surrealism is a mouthful of light a towering urge to mangle the language to beat it into tungsten a raging river fastened to the hood of a jeep old clocks yawning in oysters oracular ore at the core of an oar a Martian umbrella dressed in music." Olson has produced four full-length collections of poetry to date, preponderantly in the form of prose poetry. He has also written a novel, *Souls of Wind*, which fantasizes the life of Rimbaud. In 2008, a volume of Olson's new and selected poems, entitled *Backscatter*, was published by Black Widow Press (an important new publisher of neo-surrealist and classical surrealist writings).

Against affirmation, the poetry of Garrett Caples is at once informed by surrealism and (pace Olson) involved in wordplay, manifesting a laughingly dark umor (a paradoxical condition, first defined by Jacques Vaché, in which the power of death is reclaimed for amor). In *The Garrett Caples Reader* (1999) and in *Complications* (2007), Caples proves himself the trickster at every level of the poetic act, taxing the sins of syntax and turning the merely semantic mantic, as in the snakelike slyness of his phrase "Turning on the Tongue" (the title of a poem in *Complications*). Especially in his poems with short lines, Caples goes round with sound to found and confound meaning: "i nose / for noise," he confesses in "Dub Song of Prufrock Shakur." In phrases like "lamplit armpit" and "sup on pus," Caples bathes in high bathos, tickling the ridiculous until it sublimes. As the poet avers in "Gauntlet of Two" (from *The Garrett Caples Reader*): "It was simply a case of lost absolutes. A game of cat and mouth."

Noah Eli Gordon is the most protean and prolific of the younger poets oriented toward neo-surrealism; his first book, *The Frequencies*, was published in 2003 and he has already garnered several major awards for his writing. Gordon's poetic prestidigitations are rapid and adroit as that of a master mesmerist, conjuring a mix of voices, alternately haunting and hinting obliquely, out of thin air.

Eric Baus, another of this cohort, sees with one eye of innocence and one eye of experience, observant of the fabulations, intricate and true, found inside discarded boxes of narrative. Baus's first book, *The To Sound*, appeared in 2004.

The poetry of Sandra Simonds, whose first book, *Warsaw Bikini*, was published in 2008, is characterized by a fierce and rampant negativity that suddenly veers sideways to display a pataphysics of redemption, wickedly wise.

The work of Karen Volkman is suffused with the disquieting harmonies of a late-Symbolist aesthetics that often overspills, as did the work of Mallarmé, into surrealist alterity. Her most recent book, *Nomina* (2008), is comprised of sonnets in the form of sonic force-fields, rippling with philosophical sensations.

Christine Hume's neo-surrealist poetry is charged with the dark energies of Lautréamont and Michaux, transposed into an American vernacular. She is the author of three volumes to date: *Musca Domestica, Alaskaphrenia* (2004), and *Shot* (2010). In her writings, Hume contemplates, even as she creates, a crisis of the object of language. Her surrealism is as lawless, and as reasoned, as that of Maldoror.

Brian Lucas is the author of *Light House* (2006), a book of marvels reported with quiet yet baroque conviction, whose centerpiece is the long poem entitled "The Head in Spring," sighted on a "black hole in the sun."

Other names may be added to this roster (in random order): Andrew Zawacki, Joshua Marie Wilkinson, Brian Strang, Roberto Harrison, Heller Levinson, André Spears, et des autres encore inconnus.

As I am mindful of the struggles that will be faced by the poetry of the Imagination in the harsh century ahead, perhaps it is well to conclude this hasty résumé with the words of René Char, surrealist apprentice and resistance fighter, who wished "to keep in reserve the inaccessible as a free field for the fantasy of its suns, and resolved to pay the price for this."

JANUARY 2010

ANDREW JORON

Born in 1955, Andrew Joron was raised in Stuttgart, Germany, Lowell, MA, and Missoula, MT. He attended the University of California at Berkeley to study with the anarchist philosopher Paul Feyerabend, graduating with a degree in the philosophy of science. After a decade and a half spent writing science-fiction poetry, culminating in his volume *Science Fiction* (1992), Joron turned to a more speculative form of lyric, influenced by German Romanticism and surrealism, and reflecting his association with Philip Lamantia. This later work has been collected in *The Removes* (1999) and in *Fathom* (2003). *The Cry at Zero*, a selection of his prose poems and critical essays, was published by Counterpath Press in 2007. *Trance Archive: New & Selected Poems* was published by City Lights in 2010. Joron is also the translator, from the German, of the Marxist-Utopian philosopher Ernst Bloch's *Literary Essays* (1998). Joron's latest poetry collection is *The Sound Mirror*, published by Flood Editions. He lives in Berkeley, where he works as a part-time proofreader and indexer. He also plays Theremin in the improvisational trio Free Rein.

www.ingramcontent.com/pod-product-compliance
Lightning Source LLC
Chambersburg PA
CBHW030155070426
42447CB00032B/1210